Finding Grace

Michele P. Fuller

Copyright © 2015 Michele P. Fuller

All rights reserved.

ISBN-10: 0692481516
ISBN-13: 978-0692481516

Dedication

This book is dedicated to my coach who pushes me to dream big and
my incredible team who works so tirelessly to make them come true,
our clients who inspire us to do our very best for them,
my parents who believe I can do anything,
and my lovely children who make it all worthwhile.

Contents

About the Author

Introduction

Chapter One: The Unexpected   5

Chapter Two: A World Turned Upside Down   11

Chapter Three: Seeking Sincerity From Strangers   17

Chapter Four: A Caring Advocate   27

Chapter Five: A Place of Hope   37

Chapter Six: Newly Found Grace   45

About the Author

Michele P. Fuller is the founder of Michigan Law Center, P.L.L.C. located in Sterling Heights, Michigan. The practice focuses on elder law, special needs planning, Veteran's Administration planning and settlement planning, including a national practice establishing Qualified Settlement Funds. She is a frequent speaker for national and statewide groups.

Michele co-authored several nationally published articles, including *Traps for the Unwary During Special Needs Trust Administration*, in Estates and Trusts Magazine, the *Future of Planning for Persons with Disabilities* which was published in the Fall 2013 edition of the NAELA Journal, and *Pooled Trusts: An Approach to Special Needs Planning for Families of Modest Means*, published in the May-June 2013 edition of BiFocal, a Journal of the ABA Commission on Law and Aging.

Parenting Magazine also named Michele *Top Special Needs Child Advocate* in 2013. She also contributed to the November 2014 edition of the Michigan State Bar Journal, Planning for a Person with Disabilities. Michele is also co-author of a book entitled *Special Needs Trusts: Protect Your Child's Financial Future, 6th Edition*.

Presently, Michele lives in southeast Michigan with her four children and giant dog. She enjoys traveling, cooking, and drinking good wine.

Introduction

For those of you feeling lost and unsure of what to do or who to contact for help and information while caring for an elderly loved one, you are not alone.

With the advancing age of the Baby Boomer population and with medical advances that allow us to live longer lives, an increasing number of people are finding themselves in challenging circumstances. They suddenly become caregivers to aging parents, siblings, spouses, and loved ones while trying to see to the needs of their own family and meet the demands of a job or career. These loved ones require increasingly more assistance with their basic daily needs and routines. They also need to be protected by their caregivers and advocates through informed decision making. Unfortunately, most are unprepared for the responsibility and uniformed to make those choices, much like Anne Schuster, the woman you will read about in this book. She found herself in a desperate situation when her mother suddenly needed around-the-clock care.

Her story is similar to the experiences of many of my clients. The reason Finding Grace was written was to be able to reach those in similar situations to Anne's, so they know they are not alone. Hopefully someone reading her story will find strength and inspiration, and perhaps understand some of the key decisions to be made along the journey.

A good elder law attorney is equipped with the specialized knowledge and resources to help someone in Anne's particular circumstances of caring for an ailing parent, and guide someone through all of the legal challenges that may arise. My passion is doing exactly that; helping protect people who need to find the right care and resources for their aging loved ones.

Many clients are unprepared for the emotional toll just making the decision to place someone in a facility can take on the decision-maker as well as the loved one who needs the care. As Anne learns in Finding Grace, a hospital or nursing facility has staff to help make decisions as to where your loved one is placed. However, their guidance might be limited to providing a list of proposed facilities. If your loved one cannot make decisions, then their patient advocate must make the decision for them. If you are the advocate and you do not tell them where you want your loved one to go, the hospital or nursing facility will choose for you. As you will see from Anne's experience, not all nursing homes are alike. There can be vast differences in nursing facilities in terms of professionalism of the staff, quality of care, structure and amenities of the facility, and level of cleanliness. Because of this, it is imperative that you take the initiative and the time to research potential nursing homes so that your loved one will be living in a facility that is best suited for him or her.

No one ever wants to watch a loved one lose their independence and perhaps their very spirit. It may be jarring to become responsible for someone else's life. The gravity of that responsibility can make one feel overwhelmed, lost, and desperate. Nonetheless, if you find yourself in a situation similar to Anne's, the best approach is not to panic. Just take a moment. Breathe. As overwhelming as it all may seem, being informed and supported will help in making the best choice under difficult circumstances. Consulting an excellent elder law attorney as quickly as possible, one who truly cares about the well being of you and your loved one, can ease the stress of the situation and set you in the right direction. In the face of difficult and heartbreaking circumstances such as Anne's and many others who are facing the same challenges, there truly is a way to regain a state of solace and grace.

The Unexpected

I never anticipated the phone call I received on that bright autumn afternoon, especially since Rose was my baby sister. Being the oldest of three children, I always naively assumed I'd never live to see this happen. My mother, Miss Betty Schuster, lived with my sister for several years, ever since my father died. I was always very grateful to Rose for taking on the responsibility, allowing me to focus on my job and the many hours it required as a program manager. My mother, or Miss Betty, as I sometimes call her, was quite the character and never ill-intended, but she could be quite a challenge. Since they lived nearby, I would often try to spend some time with my mother a couple nights a week to give Rose a much needed break.

The day I got the phone call about the accident, it was a crisp, sunny October day, and the turned leaves were just starting to free from the trees and dance through the air. I was considering raking the yard as I sipped on a cup of tea and stood staring out the back window.

Rose was driving my mother home from one of her routine doctor's appointments. My mother, who apparently was in one of her feistier moods, was not willing to hear that her salt intake needed altering.

"It looks like we might need to put away the salt shaker for a while to get your blood pressure under control a bit. Don't you think, Mom?" coaxed my sister. Being the gentle soul that she was, Rose was never one to use harsh tactics. Miss Betty, on the other hand, was another story.

"I don't see why I have to do any such thing! Life's too short to eat bland chicken!"

Rose chuckled. "A little bit is fine, Mom, but at dinner last night it was like a blizzard on your baked potato...."

The conversation apparently distracted Rose, who did not see the white SUV that ran the red light and plunged into the driver's side of the car as she was crossing the intersection. According to the responding emergency unit, my sister was dead instantly because of the speed at which the vehicle hit her side of the car and the nature of the wounds. She was only 54 years old. I can't imagine the horror my mother experienced when this happened. Miraculously, she only suffered a bad case of whiplash, several bumps and bruises, and a broken wrist, but thankfully nothing serious. She had a brief stay at the hospital to ensure she was stable, but was soon discharged.

When my mother left the hospital, it was clear she needed to stay with me, at first to deal with the trauma of losing Rose. It was difficult for me to comprehend that my sister was gone, but I kept it together the best I could for the sake of my mother. My mother was not one to show emotion in front of others, even in front of her own children. She was very quiet for days, and did not speak much of the accident or what happened in the car after they were hit, which told she was devastated. There was no way I was going to leave her alone during this time.

However, as time passed, I realized that she needed increasingly more help and it was clear that I needed to keep her with me. She had not lived on her own for several years and was starting to need assistance with the little details of her routine because the arthritis in her knees made it hard for her to get around on certain days. She was also starting to show early signs of dementia; not knowing where she put the television remote, calling me Rose instead of Anne, and accusing me of hiding her favorite necklace started to become more frequent occurrences. However, at 90 years old, I felt it was to be expected. She was otherwise her spunky, colorful self.

As time progressed, it was becoming increasingly more difficult to both care for my mother and work full time. I was running errands, setting up food for easy meals while I was gone, taking her to appointments after work or during lunch hours, and calling her frequently to ensure she was okay. However, she was becoming worse in her ability to walk around the house. I feared for her safety and could picture her falling while getting herself a cup of tea or walking to the bathroom.

Mary, my other younger sister, tried tirelessly to help in some way. She lived an hour and a half away with her husband and three grown children. Determined to help, she would drive down three days a week and check in on my mother while I was working. As much as I appreciated her concern and efforts, it still wasn't enough. But, I couldn't ask her to do more because of the drive she was already enduring. The fact was my mother needed more attention than my sister and I could give her, and we were both extremely worried that she was no longer safe spending time alone.

One afternoon, when arriving home after a three hour round-trip to see my mother, Mary phoned me.

"Hey Anne, have you ever considered an in-home caregiver? That might help fill the gaps when you or I aren't around to help Mom. She almost fell three times today, and couldn't find her slippers to save her life. I didn't feel right leaving before you were home today."

Why hadn't I thought of that? What a wonderful idea! My sister had a way of thinking of things that I never would. Mary was veterinary assistant and had the medical mind for details that I sometimes lacked. I immediately acted and called the hospital to request a part-time aid, and soon a nurse's aid named Susan came to visit on a routine basis. She took my mother to appointments, helped her get around, and assisted with anything else that was needed while I was at work or at work related functions and when my sister couldn't be there. I still was spending many hours preparing things for the day, making lists for Susan, setting up food and medication, etc., but at least my mother wasn't alone and at risk of hurting herself.

Miss Betty adored Susan. Thankfully, she was aware of the fact that she needed someone to help her, and was happy to have such a kind person with which to spend time. There were nights I would come home and find that my mother insisted on playing poker (she was adamant that Susan needed to learn how to play cards), while telling over-dramatized stories about the long list of attractive men who wanted to court her when she was young and gorgeous. In place of poker chips, they used Honey O's cereal. Needless to say, I was hopeful that this was a solid solution that would make daily life work again for everyone involved.

I had no idea of the events that would soon occur.

A World Turned Upside Down

The doctor stood before me and Mary in the hallway of the hospital in his long, white lab coat. He was tall and had perfectly styled dark hair. As I looked at him, I couldn't help but think that my mother would be flirting with him at this very moment if she were in better condition. She had a habit of shamelessly flirting with tall, attractive doctors.

"Your mother has had a series of mini-strokes, which is why she has been having severe headaches. As you mentioned, she has lost a great deal of her sight, which is also due to the strokes, but we are hoping she does not lose it completely."

"Her dementia has worsened in the last couple of weeks. Is this Alzheimer's or is it because of the strokes?" I asked.

"Your mother has vascular dementia. The symptoms are similar to Alzheimer's disease, but the dementia is the result of the damage caused by the strokes. Unfortunately, this is not reversible and will likely progress."

I felt odd, like I was in a dream. At 92, my mother's health was failing her, but she was a person that I never could picture in this state because she was such an independent, downright stubborn spirit. Now, she couldn't see, eat on her own, or remember that my name is Anne.

The hallway in which we stood was uncomfortably quiet and the rooms that lined the hallway were filled with people coping with similar issues as my mother. Being in the veterinary field, my sister had medical questions of which I would never think to ask. I was vaguely aware of her conversation with the doctor, which sounded more like a low hum in the background. My mind wandered a moment as I wondered if doctors ever got used to giving people horrible news about their loved ones. It must be one of the most difficult parts of their profession, I thought, to look at people in the eyes and tell them exactly what they don't want to hear about someone they love.

After another full day of tests and evaluations, I took my mother home, wondering how I was going to take care of her under the circumstances. I had absolutely no idea how to make this happen. Even worse, I lacked the knowledge of the resources that could possibly help my mother and I. I was completely overwhelmed as my mind raced with questions I had no idea how to answer. Do I keep her home and pay an in-home caregiver? What would that cost? Is it covered by my mother's Medicare? Or, is it better to place her in a nursing home? How do I do that, and how is that covered financially? Are there waiting lists to get into nursing facilities? I wondered who would have the answers to these questions. A lawyer? I could not even think of a word that would describe the kind of lawyer I needed. The title "elder law attorney" was not one of which I had heard in the past.

I took several days off from work to take care of my mother and to figure out what exactly I was going to do, and it was immediately clear that she needed constant help. She was partially blind and her sight was worsening by the day. As a result, for her to eat, I needed to guide her hand to the plate or glass. Furthermore, she could not stand and walk without support, and, once she was standing, her lack of sight made it even more difficult for her. Essentially, I became Miss Betty's eyes and legs, and that is how we got through those first days at home.

Meanwhile, I was frantically trying to find help. After some research, I realized that bringing in full-time help to the house was not an option, being that I could barely afford the part-time help with Susan. Paying thousands more a month was definitely something I could not do.

Making matters more difficult was the fact that my mother started having issues with incontinence, and I was cleaning and changing her pants and undergarments several times throughout the day. I was having a hard time keeping up with constantly changing the linens. Just keeping her clean and dry was becoming all-consuming. I was becoming exhausted mentally and physically.

One morning, I woke and realized that my mother was still sleeping, which was unusual because she was a lifelong early riser and was typically up and about well before the break of dawn. At this point, she needed me to help her out of bed and would usually call for me to help her do so. However, this particular morning, I heard nothing. When I walked into her room, she was partially awake, groggy, and very lethargic. I felt a heated surge of panic briefly run through my body.

"Rose, I don't feel like getting up yet," said my mother as I tried to remove her soiled pajama pants and give her clean clothing. The smell of her urine was pungent and overwhelming the room. "I don't want to do this. I'm exhausted, honey, and it hurts down here when I move around," pointing to her lower abdomen. At this point, any new ache, pain, or symptom of any kind was frightening to me. I worried about what these new symptoms might mean and feared the worst. What was happening now and why?

Once she refused to eat, I called her doctor immediately. Again, we found ourselves in the emergency room and my mother was quickly admitted. She was suffering from a bladder infection so severe that it was affecting her cognitive ability and worsening her dementia. Again, I found myself walking the hushed halls of the hospital, waiting for answers about my mother and desperately hoping I would somehow know what to do next. After much pacing and thought, it was clear in my mind that I needed professional advice to make sure I took care of matters in the right manner, for my mother and for myself. I wouldn't be able to sleep at night if I made a mistake that affected my mother's well being. It was critical that I do this right. I decided at that moment, in the quiet corridors of the hospital, that I definitely needed an attorney.

Seeking Sincerity From Strangers

My mother was in the hospital for two weeks, as the doctors tried to stabilize her and rid her of the infection. Her appetite began to return, along with her energy, but the dementia was progressively becoming worse.

The nursing staff would coax her onto her feet at least three times a day and walk with her around the room and hallways. Sometimes I would assist her while she slowly and carefully moved her legs, step by step, using the walker as her guide. As with the dementia, her sight was worsening. This required someone to help her when it was time for her to eat, which I often did. She would repeatedly talk to me, not knowing it was me.

"Rose honey, could you give me another spoonful of that soup?" she would ask, as her arthritic fingers searched for the glass of water. I didn't correct her. There was no reason to upset her.

Essentially, after two weeks in the hospital, there was nothing she could do on her own. So, it was no surprise when the hospital informed me that they would need to discharge her to a nursing home for continued physical and occupational therapy.

This made me think of the fact that I had yet to find an attorney, and was having a difficult time doing so. As I said before, I wasn't exactly sure what I needed. I didn't even know what questions to ask or where to begin. What kind of lawyer would best suit this situation? A disability lawyer didn't seem to be a fit; they seemed to deal with those who had suffered accidents and were seeking settlements. I needed someone who specialized in my mother's exact situation to help me make smart financial and legal choices for her. I suddenly realized that I needed this lawyer as quickly as possible for the situation became even more complicated when the head nurse approached me.

"At this point, your mother needs to be discharged directly to a nursing home for continued rehabilitation," she said as she flipped through several pages of paper in her hands.

"Where is she going?" I asked.

"This particular home is only two blocks away and is quite lovely inside. We discharge people to this facility often," she said, as she handed me information pertaining to the nursing home. I flipped through a pamphlet that had large colored pictures of the home's designer decor. A grand piano in the lobby was featured on the front cover. Honestly, it did look lovely, and it was located in an affluent area, which led me to believe that it must be a reliable place to take her.

"How does she pay for this? Is it covered by her Medicare?" I asked, aware of the fact that I sounded incredibly ignorant to the process, which, in fact, I was.

"She was in the hospital for 14 days, which qualifies her for Medicare coverage at the nursing home. She should have 20 days of Medicare allowed to her by law in the nursing home. We will be discharging her Wednesday. I will get the discharge information for you," she said as she left my mother's room.

It all seemed to happen so quickly and emphatically, and the nurse seemed so well-informed, that I never once thought to question the information about Medicare. However, what were we going to do once those 20 days were over, and was there an alternative facility that might be more affordable? I decided to talk to one of the hospital social workers to help me with the answers.

The social worker the hospital assigned to me suggested that I look into eventually putting my mother into a group home. Again, I knew nothing about group homes and began to quickly research the idea. She gave me the name of several group homes in the area, so I decided to visit one.

That evening, I drove to the closest home on the list. It only took one visit to know, without a doubt, that a group home was not for my mother. I am not sure what the social worker was thinking. My mother could not walk on her own, nor could she see. As I strolled through the facility, I saw immediately that there were no hand rails or grab bars in the bathroom facilities, no tub benches or roll-in showers, and the place was laden with stairways to climb. This would never work. I was beginning to realize that I could not rely on hospital staff or social workers to make decisions for my mother, no matter how well-informed or well-intentioned they might appear to be.

Consequently, I started wondering how accurate the hospital was about the nursing home to which my mother was headed on Wednesday, and how accurate the information was about Medicare. My mind started to become overwhelmed with worry. Every answer or direction I received so far seemed to lead to more questions and more confusion.

That night I called Mary to inform her of what happened that day, giving her all of the details about the nursing home, Medicare, the group home, and all of my concerns. It felt good to talk to someone with sincerity in her voice, someone who cared, especially after listening to strangers for days.

Mary agreed that I needed to consult an attorney, but she was not sure who exactly I should call, especially since she and her husband did not live anywhere close to where I was located.

"Let me ask John. He might have a good idea of someone in your area." replied Mary. Her husband was a corporate attorney in East Lansing and I was hopeful that he might know someone who could help.

The next morning, I made my way to the hospital. It was the day my mother was going to be discharged. When

I entered the room, she smiled at me. She seemed to be in a chipper mood

"Good morning," she said as she flipped through a travel magazine one of the nurses must have given her. "Honey, can you hand me my glasses? I can't see a darn thing."

She forgot that reading glasses were not going to help her. Not having the heart to dampen her cheerful mood, I quickly changed the subject.

"Well, Miss Betty, today is the day that we are going to the new facility, and it's supposed to be very nice." Just as I finished my statement, the social worker entered the room and immediately began to speak.

"Oh good, you're here. So that you can make the appropriate plans, I wanted you to know that your mother is not eligible for aid beyond the 20 days at the facility to which you are taking her today."

My stomach seemed to ball up into my throat. "How is that possible? No aid at all?" I replied.

"Unfortunately, your mother has too many assets to qualify for aid," she said.

"Too many assets? My mother does not have much at all. Her money would be depleted within months without help."

"I'm sorry – I hate to be the bearer of bad news. You can look into this more. Maybe there are other options for her."

Her phone rang and she excused herself to take the call. How could she have too many assets? My mother was by no means financially well-off. She had a relatively small amount of money in her checking and savings account that came to about $15,000 in total, and a modest investment account of almost $40,000. I could not believe that those figures would stop her from qualifying for aid. If that were true, what were we going to do?

My mind was racing as I drove my mother to the new facility. The situation was becoming overwhelming. Thankfully, my mother seemed to understand why she was going to the new facility and she was not upset by the idea. So far, the one aspect of my mother's circumstances for which I was grateful was that she had received excellent care and remained content and in good spirits.

Getting my mother out of the car and into the lobby of the nursing home was a laborious process. As she used her walker, I guided her up the ramp and into the building. The pictures of the nursing home proved accurate as we walked through the lobby to the front desk. Because my mother moved slowly, I was able to take a good look around before reaching the receptionist. The ceilings were vaulted with ornate, white crown moldings throughout the structure. Enormous windows encased the room, causing the buffed marble floors to reflect the beaming sun. Of course, the show case was the large, black grand piano featured on the pamphlet I read earlier.

However, among all of the pomp and circumstance of the room, the one thing that struck me was the smell. There was a tang of sourness in the air, a smell I knew too well, and it immediately made me uneasy.

The receptionist called for an administrator to help finish the rest of the paperwork and settle my mother into her room. The nurse, who introduced herself as Vickie, also joined us to help. She was unemotional in her demeanor, even cold at times, and I was hoping that there was a softer interior to what met the eyes. I helped my mother walk to the dining room area that was connected to an additional area with couches and a large television, and I spent lunchtime with her as she ate.

"So what do you think so far, Mom?"

"The place seems harmless enough…except for Vickie. That's a tough nut." I chuckled. "Well, if anyone can crack it, it's you." Miss Betty laughed.

The next morning, I visited my mother on my way to work, leaving early enough so that I could spend some time with her. I couldn't help but feel heartsick and worried about her, even though there was very little concrete information to which I could connect my emotions. Nonetheless, I couldn't shake the gut feeling.

My mother was already up and sitting alone in the dining room area. Her food and water bottle were untouched, mainly because she couldn't see to feed herself or grab the bottle. I immediately began to help her, not knowing how long she had been sitting there. She was incredibly thirsty, and drank all of her water quickly.

It was also apparent that she had wet herself and had been sitting in her own urine for some time. The bitter scent was unmistakable. Anger was growing within me and I immediately went to find someone to assist my mother.

Thankfully, a nurse was right around the corner.

"Excuse me," I said to her. I must have startled her because she turned with a jolt. "I didn't mean to sneak up on you like that, but my mother needs assistance. I'm not sure how long she's been sitting here alone in this condition."

She looked over at my mother. "Betty hasn't been there long. I just walked her out here about 30 minutes ago," she replied as she walked over to my mother. It was clear to me that she failed to see the problem, even though my mother's needs were specifically discussed the previous day with the administrator and the nurse.

Feeling uneasy about her aloof response, I again explained my mother's issues and needs, hoping she would be more helpful to her. However, as the days unfolded, there seemed to be a different nurse watching over my mother every time I came to visit. One nurse, whose name was Gina, was incredibly attentive and I could tell my mother enjoyed her. She smiled when Gina sat and helped her, and talked about "what a doll" she was.

Unfortunately, the remaining nurses I encountered were not as accommodating. For instance, on the third day of my mother's stay, I noticed that she had been drinking a lot of water and most likely had to use the bathroom, but her nurse, who happened to be Vickie that day, was nowhere to be seen. When she finally came to her room, I mentioned to her that my mother should probably use the bathroom.

"She's fine," she responded, cutting me off. "I just had her use the bathroom a little while ago." Her words were quick and jagged as she turned and left the room. I felt heat shoot through my chest, angered that someone would tell me what my own mother did or did not need.

"She's always rude. I haven't seen that woman crack a smile yet! Must be exhausting!" declared my mother.

As a result, my mother ended up wetting herself shortly after she left the room. Vickie would not make eye contact with me as I helped her clean my mother and change her clothes.

By the fourth day at the facility, it was clear to me that no matter how beautiful the facility appeared, the care was substandard and unacceptable. I felt guilty leaving her there in the evenings, unsure of what I would find in the morning. Nights were spent sleepless with worry. It was eating away at me that my mother wasn't being treated in the manner that she deserved and so desperately needed in her deteriorating state.

However, I never expected the call I received on that day from the administrator of the nursing home. She was quick worded and to the point, as if this was everyday information, like the weather or lunch specials. I was told that they could not help my mother any further, and that she had "plateaued," as the woman described it. She added that her Medicare days at the nursing home were ending and that I needed to privately pay for care or take her home immediately. For a moment, I was silent.

"I'm not sure I understand." Frozen and stunned, it was all I could think of saying.

"It would be good if you came in to either make

arrangements to take her home, or to work out the private pay terms."

I don't remember much of what I said at that point and we both hung up. I sat, staring forward for a brief second.

What instantly followed changed the entire course of events.

My phone rang again, as if responding to the previous call. A rush of relief washed over me when I heard my sister's voice on the other end.

"Anne, I have a name and number for you. Her name is Michele Fuller and, from what I've been told, she is an exceptional eldercare attorney. She's who you need, Anne."

A Caring Advocate

My sister's husband read a recent article Michele Fuller wrote in the Michigan Bar Journal. Impressed by the article, he knew immediately who I should call when Mary approached him. As professionally accomplished and renowned as Michele was, sincerity and kindness were deeply woven within the tone of her voice, and I immediately liked her and felt at ease when I spoke to her on the phone.

"We absolutely need to resolve this as quickly as possible for you and your mother," Michele said in response to hearing the situation. "Is it possible for you to come to my office today?"

"Yes, that would be ideal," I said, intuitively knowing I had finally found someone with my mother's best interest at heart.

We worked out a time in the afternoon, and before we hung up, Michele made one critical point.

"Whatever you do, do NOT take your mother out of the nursing home, no matter what they tell you. I will explain more of the details when we meet, but it is extremely important that you keep her there at the moment. It is very, very difficult to find nursing home placement from a person's home. There are usually extremely long waiting lists for community members—people living at home—that need nursing home care."

"I did not know that. So I really could have created a terrible situation if I would have done what the nursing home said to do?"

"Absolutely. The best way to get into a nursing home is to be discharged from the hospital directly to the nursing home of your choice. The second best way is to be transferred from your current facility to the nursing home of your choice. I will explain how we are going to make this happen….Take a deep breath, Anne. Things are going to work out. See you soon!"

When I walked into Michele's office, I felt the same sense of calm and warmth as I did when I heard her voice on the phone. After entering through the glass doors, the receptionist cordially directed me into a conference room that was decorated with an artist's eye. A vintage looking clock hung on the wall next to me, and on the opposite wall were two large decorative keys, ornately scrolled and painted in a manner that spoke to antiquity and tradition.

Michele did not keep me waiting as she entered the conference room with her paralegal, Erin, shook my hand with big smiles from both of them, and sat down across from me. I told her how wonderful it was to meet her and to finally have someone on my mother's "team," as I put it. As she spoke, there was a softness to her, yet strength in her attitude and speech.

"That I am," she said with a smile. "So we know that we need to keep her in the nursing home at the moment. Let me explain a few things so that you will understand what I think is a smart course of action. What you were told—that your mother qualifies for 20 days of Medicare in the home—is not true."

"Really?" I responded.

"Yes. Actually, your mother qualifies for up to 100 days of Medicare coverage. After 20 days, there is a twenty percent co-pay."

I couldn't believe it. "Then why are they telling me now that Medicare won't cover her anymore, after only five days?"

"The nursing home told Medicare that they cannot help her anymore, which caused Medicare to stop any further payments to the nursing home. Sadly, I see this all of the time."

"Why would the nursing home do this?" I asked.

"Many times nursing homes will discharge a patient from skilled nursing care covered by Medicare on the basis that the patient is failing to improve. This if often referred to as "plateauing.""

Erin nodded in agreement. "You would not believe how often this happens," she added.

Michele leaned forward as she spoke. "However, plateauing is not a valid reason to end Medicare coverage.

Not knowing this fact, many people in your position accept this information and move on to privately pay the nursing home for care, or take their loved one home."

I never would have known this if it weren't for Michele. Who would ever think that a nursing facility would do something like this to people who truly needed help?

"But now, they are receiving no payment at all and my mother's still there. Does this mean I have to take her out immediately?" I asked.

"Absolutely not. They cannot just kick your mother out, Anne. They do not have legal right to do that. Actually, they have an obligation to allow you to find proper care, and even assist you if you ask. Usually, there is up to 30 days allotted for these arrangements to be made. That being said, we have to make decisions quickly and find a place where she will be well cared for and be able to stay long-term."

I was incredibly relieved to hear these words. Although 30 days wasn't much time, I at least had the opportunity to find a place for my mother.

The afternoon was incredibly productive and informative, as the details of my mother's finances were then discussed. I informed Michele of the figures concerning her checking, savings, and investment accounts so that she could work on calculations.

As is, if my mother privately paid the nursing home, she would have been drained of all of her assets in eight months. My mind started swimming with the reality of that situation. What would happen after all of the money was gone? Would I have to pay for the nursing home? What if she needed additional help? How would I pay for her funeral? The frantic questions in my mind were endless. However, we were now on a path that would never allow for that to happen.

To solve this problem, Michele came up with a carefully thought-out plan, and she began to explain the plan by stating that it is imperative that I find a nursing home that will accept Medicaid.

"Not all nursing homes accept Medicaid," added Michele, "which many people do not realize. Anne, in your search, it is critical that the nursing home you choose does participate in the Medicaid program, and I'll tell you why."

Again, I felt so relieved that I found someone who not only cared about our situation, but who took the time to explain the reasoning behind the plan so that I understood the importance of certain details and decisions. Because of this, I could feel the stress leaving me.

Her explanation was very clear, and it shed light on why she was going to implement with me the next course of action. She was going to help my mother qualify for Medicaid assistance and save at least part of my parent's life savings. The first thing she advised me to do was to purchase an irrevocable pre-paid funeral for my mother. She advised that making my funeral arrangements was a valid way to spend down her funds. It was very difficult to think of having to make these arrangements for my mother, and I could feel my eyes water and threaten to overflow. Michele sensed this and paused, handing me a tissue. She reassured me that she understood this was a difficult thing she was asking me to do.

Next, Michele explained a detailed plan of action that would be able to save some of my parent's hard-earned money. Due to her medical costs there wasn't much left, but anything we could save for her was better than nothing. Miss Betty had always been insistent that she wanted to leave as much as she could to her girls. But, Mary and I were fine financially. We were worried about our mother's care and quality of life. She loved her house and the lifetime of memories it had for her. The fear of losing her house to the State was something Mary and I had heard about and would try to prevent if at all possible. Michele explained that Medicaid is the government program that helps people to need long-term care, but you have to financially qualify to be eligible.

Michele explained that in order to qualify for Long-Term Care Medicaid assistance, we needed to reduce her countable assets to $2,000. She then went on to explain in detail what we needed to do, and why. I was given a detailed list of what Michele would need. I was relieved to learn that the state would not "take" my childhood home and there was a way to pass it along to me and Mary after my mother was gone. We would even be able to avoid the probate process, which would make things easy for us after my mother's inevitable passing, which I could barely allow myself to contemplate. However, I knew sharing this information with Miss Betty would give her peace of mind to the extent she could understand what was going on. I know my sister would feel better as well knowing my parent's wishes would be honored. I felt immensely relieved, and knew we were in good hands. It was unbelievable. Michele described exactly what I had been experiencing with the care providers and gave me sound advice on how to respond. I finally had what I needed: answers to my questions, and a plan of action, and confidence that I could make my mother's situation change for the better.

When our meeting was finished, I drove directly from Michele's office to the bank that held my mother's accounts. Thankfully, after my sister died, my mother and I had the foresight to make arrangements with the bank for both of us to have joint control of her finances.

When I reached the bank, I wrote three checks, just as Michele advised. The first and most important one was the check to retain Michele as our attorney. My family needed her in our corner. Writing those three checks felt empowering, knowing that it was my first step to truly protecting my mother.

The next step was to find a nursing home for my mother, one that would not only take excellent care of her but would also accept Medicaid. However, before I began my search, I stopped at the nursing home to check on Miss Betty, who was sitting alone, again, with two full water bottles in front of her.

"Hi Mom," I said softly, so not to startle her. With her sight almost completely gone, I was a shadowy figure standing in front of her, and she almost looked past me as she spoke.

"Oh, honey, could you please help me. I am so thirsty and I don't know where they put the water," she asked in a distressed tone.

I moved the bottles closer to her and directed her hand toward one of them. Her hand slightly shook as she held the bottle to her mouth, quickly drinking half of it, then the rest of it, as if she had just spent a long, hot summer day in the sun. It broke my heart that she could no longer do such a thing, and that she had to spend her time in a place like this. I wondered how long she was sitting there wanting to drink but without help to do so. Knowing that I was going to find a better place was the only thing that eased the pain and guilt of leaving her there that night. After meeting with Michele, I knew I could change my mother's circumstances quickly.

Before leaving, I let the woman at the main desk know that I was planning on moving my mother to a new facility, and that I would keep them informed as to when this will happen as soon as I find the facility. The information I gained from Michele made me realize that, in reality, I am in control of this situation as my mother's power of attorney, which caused me to speak concisely and with confidence. Armed with legally accurate information, I was no longer afraid or worried to assert myself.

That night, I looked into possible facilities close to my own home. There were two in particular that looked interesting, and I called the main desk of each to ensure that they did accept Medicaid. Michele had stressed that I needed to find a place that made it easy for me to visit my mother, especially during our harsh winter months. She also said that the more frequently I visit my mother, the better her care will be. I was surprised to hear her talk about me and my life as well, and how important it was to take care of myself and not push myself to exhaustion and having my mother close by would be a comfort to me, knowing I could drop in at any time, even after a long day at work.

After leaving my mother, later that night I called my sister to thank her for giving me Michele's number and let her know about the plan and the information I had received from Michele. She was as relieved as I was that the situation, as dire as it was, made a 180 degree turn in just one day. Retaining Michele as my mother's attorney completely changed the course of events.

During my lunch hour the next day, Mary drove down to meet with me so we could visit the two nursing homes together. From what I read, the first home we visited, Chelsea Care Center, received mixed ratings based on our internet searches, but I thought it might be worthwhile to take a look at it for ourselves.

One thing I had learned from this experience was that one should never judge a nursing facility by its appearance and fancy décor. I now had a new perspective on the details of which to take careful note. Michele recommended I look for accommodations, such as hand rails and grab bars. Were people active and getting the attention they needed? Was it clean? Were there fowl odors? Were people smiling and interacting or were they upset and isolated? Were they wearing their glasses? Do they have their teeth in? These were things I would never have thought to look for.

When Mary and I walked through the Chelsea Care Center, we noticed that many of the people were alone in their rooms, strapped to their wheelchairs to prevent them from standing. Many of them appeared dazed and drugged. We walked past the room of a woman who was rocking herself and yelling. Her hair was ratted and gray, and the unmistakable smell of urine hit me as I walked past.

Mary looked my way. Her light blue eyes were filled with heartbreak and worry.

"I can tell you right now, there is no way I want Mom in this place," she said. "I have worked in kennels that have substantially better care than what I am seeing here."

I agreed with her. There was an intangible feeling both my sister and I experienced as we briefly walked through the facility. It was a somber feeling, one laden with depression, and I felt deeply disturbed by the surroundings. Needless to say, we left, feeling heartsick that the people who lived in the home couldn't do the same. I knew we could never put our mother in a place like this.

Being that our visit to the Chelsea Care Center was so short-lived, we had plenty of time to visit the second nursing home on our list, named Gateway Manor. My hopes were high that this might be the place where my mother would find solace.

A Place of Hope

As I walked through the second nursing home with my sister, there was a completely different quality to its atmosphere. This was a very different scene from which we came, one that was filled with the heavy scent of soiled clothing and disturbing views of drugged and dazed elderly alone in their rooms.

Being that it was lunchtime, many of the patients were in the dining and lounge area in the front of the building. Most were grouped in the dining room while they ate, to encourage a social environment. The people were smiling and talking to each other. I even heard laughing. There were several nurses and aids in the area to care for the patients, as I watched them rush in and out of the room, giving food to people, cleaning trays, and feeding those who needed help. From around a corner, another nurse came in pushing a middle-aged woman who was in what appeared to be a catatonic state. My eyes followed the nurse as she wheeled the woman to one of the groups, allowing her to be a member of the social activity. My sister stood next to me and also silently watched.

"How impressive that they make sure she is a part of the conversation," Mary said quietly, so that only I could hear. "They are making sure she gets to hear the discussions and reap the benefits of the cognitive stimulation even though she is unresponsive."

The people who were in the group were not at all uncomfortable with her presence, and included her in the conversation with the acknowledgment that she could possibly hear them. We both agreed that the sight of her sitting in that small group, as those around her enjoyed the soup and chatted, was both impressive and moving.

I asked the receptionist if I could take a moment to stroll around parts of the facility that were open to visitors, and she kindly responded that I certainly could. Thankfully, this particular facility was built to be wheelchair accessible, and also included the different types of bars and rails throughout the building needed by those who have trouble moving on their own.

The décor was simple and modest, with a fresh coat of paint on the walls and a spotless tan carpet. There were no ornate crown moldings, vaulted ceilings, or grand pianos. However, it was neat and, most impressively, clean. The air smelled like chicken soup, warm buttered bread, and freshly laundered clothes.

Most importantly, the view I had as I watched the hustle and hum of a Tuesday at noon showed people who actually enjoyed one another. They weren't only people who could no longer take care of themselves. At that moment, I was looking at a room full of friends.

I left work early that day and returned to Gateway Manor to speak to the admissions director, Janice Smith. Mary and I were convinced that this was the nursing home for our mother, and I wanted to make this happen for her as quickly as possible. When I met Janice, it was clear that she was a kind, well informed woman who appreciated a no-nonsense approach to situations, which I found refreshing. As I sat in her small office, I let her know that I was currently working with an elder law attorney who is helping my mother plan and apply for Medicaid assistance. In fact, after I shared that I was working with Michele's firm, Janice's demeanor went from merely informative to positively warm. She said that they had worked with Michele and assured me that I was dealing with a firm with an excellent reputation. It was no surprise to learn that the nursing facility had a good opinion of Michele's firm and their work, but it just reinforced the fact that Mary and I had chosen the right lawyer to work with to protect our mother.

"That is ideal," she said, as her eyes lit up. "To increase the likelihood of your mother's acceptance into the home, I need a letter from the firm verifying that you are in the process of applying for Medicaid benefits. If I can get that letter in hand, I can then take it to accounting to prove that your mother is financially a 'low risk' patient to the nursing home and that she has an attorney handling the paperwork."

She could tell by the look on my face that I did not

fully understand what "low risk" meant.

"In other words," she continued, "the home is assured that it will be promptly paid and that the process would be expedited due to an informed attorney."

Immediately upon leaving the nursing home, I called Michele's office and informed Michele of the letter. She knew exactly what I needed.

"Absolutely, Anne. That's part of our standard operating procedure. I'll have it to you by the morning."

She was true to her word, as she was throughout the entire process. The next morning I received the letter, which was quite simple, essentially stating that Michele has been retained as my attorney and that she was handling the Medicaid application process. That morning, I was able to take the letter back to Janice, who then took it straight to the accounting department. As a result, within a day, the home accepted my mother.

Furthermore, because of the assurance of Medicaid assistance, I was informed that I did not have to pay the entire first month's fees for security measures, which would have been $10,000. Instead, I only had to pay a portion of the fee to cover the difference in the time it took for the Medicaid payment to reach the nursing home. In the end, I only had to pay $600, which is much less of a burden than $10,000.

Finally, it was time to move my mother to Gateway Manor. It was almost hard to believe that, within days, our dire situation was not only resolved, but had blossomed into a result that was more than I could have envisioned or hoped for my mother. The feeling of achievement was overwhelming, and it was a direct result of Michele's sound legal advice, careful planning, and sincere care for me and my mother. Because of Michele and her legal team, Miss Betty was finally going to receive the care she needed.

When I entered the nursing home the next afternoon, I was instantly reminded of why I was relieved that she was leaving. Once again, my mother was sitting alone, this time in her room. She was strapped to a wheelchair, apparently to ensure that she could not move from it. There were three water bottles around her, all full and untouched, and the room was filled with a pungent stench. My mother had been sitting in her own waste for what seemed to be quite some time. I was appalled at the quality of care my mother was receiving and wanted nothing more than to clean her up and get her out of there as soon as possible.

The anger that boiled within me caused me to clean my mother on my own. If I actually talked to one of the nurses, I might have completely lost my temper.

"Thank you, hon, for helping me. These people here are rude. Can you believe that they chained me to this chair? What am I? An animal?" my mother said. There were pockets of time that, when she spoke, it was as if the dementia never existed.

"We are leaving this place, Mom. I found a new nursing home that I think you are going to like very much. The people there seem wonderful," I said to her as I finished helping her put on her clothes.

"We're leaving today?" she asked. Her voice was filled with the hope of a child.

"Yep! Right after I gather your things. The place is called Gateway Manor, and it is much different than this place. You will be able to sit with the other people that live there and enjoy yourself."

My mother smiled at me. "Whatever you do, Anne, don't forget to pack my lucky deck of cards."

Being that my mother had not spent much time at the nursing home, she did not have much to pack. Thankfully, we were ready to go without much effort. I informed the woman at the front desk that my mother was leaving with me. There were three nurses, including Vickie, who stood nearby and heard my conversation with the receptionist. I found it interesting that they did not react in any way as I stood and signed the papers. No one said goodbye to my mother, or wished her well. Not even a smile. The cold, callous air was palpable.

I struggled as I attempted to push my mother's wheelchair through the doors to reach my car that was parked in front of the large windows, and, again, not one person moved to help in my struggle. Likewise, getting my mother into the car took great effort, and yet those inside simply stood and observed.

As we slowly drove away, without realizing it at first, my mother and I had the same natural reaction. In an unstaged, synchronized manner, we both took in a deep breath and released. As I exhaled, it was as if the intense stress that built within was leaving me, blown into the air, and disbursed. Most importantly, it was clear that my mother felt the same.

Newly Found Grace

Today, I can sleep soundly at night knowing I did all that I could to create the exact circumstances my mother needs. At Gateway Manor, the nurses and staff are not only attentive and professional, but they genuinely like my mother and care about her well being. One nurse in particular, a tall man in his early 40's, plays a game of poker with my mother every day after lunch as she shamelessly flirts with him. Once the game ends, he makes sure she takes her medication and has everything she needs.

"See you tomorrow, Miss Betty. Meanwhile, try to stay out of trouble, okay?" he usually says to her, with a warm smile. He then notifies the nurse that is assigned to her during the next shift that he is leaving.

I visit my mother every day, either during my lunch hour or after work, during the dinner hour. When I walk in, her eyes are bright and smiling and there is a nurse helping her find her water and food so that she may eat her meal with ease. The room is sun-filled and there is always the hum of light conversation floating throughout the air.

"Meet my friend Martha," my mother said to me at lunch today, as she touched the arm of the elderly woman sitting in a wheelchair next to her, who also had a big smile and was very appreciative to say hello. "Martha, this is my daughter, Anne...."

In the end, because of Michele's involvement in the approval process, my mother qualified for Medicaid assistance within three months, as opposed to eight months, which saved her thousands of dollars.

Furthermore, Michele's intelligent and thoughtful planning saved a large portion of my mother's assets, allowing me to keep some of my mother's funds to help pay for any of her needs not covered by Medicaid. I can now pay for my mother to have her hair done once a week, which she absolutely loves. I also bought her new eyeglasses after an updated eye exam and I have her dental work done on a routine basis. I even bought her all new pajamas and bedding so that that she feels comfortable and confident in her new home. However, her favorite new item I was able to afford with the money saved is a new iPad to help her communicate with the staff, friends and family.

None of this would be happening without Michele Fuller and her team of legal professionals. This point speaks to a main lesson in my experience, a lesson I will never forget. No matter how much I felt that I was alone and lost, it didn't have to be that way. I was not alone. There was an exceptional elder law attorney who was more than willing to inform my decisions as well as cause procedures to flow smoothly for me and my mother. All it took was one phone call to Michele for our lives to change for the better.

Through Michele's thoughtful, meticulous planning and careful calculations tailored to our unique situation, I now have a prepaid funeral for my mother and Medicaid assistance that allows my mother to live in the nursing home of our choice. Furthermore, the nursing home in which my mother presently lives would most likely not have been an option without Michele's invaluable knowledge, instruction and continual support as to how to handle the situation at each stage, each critical decision.

Likewise, I was not aware of the extent of advocacy someone needs at key decision points, especially when someone is being discharged to a facility. If I did not have Michele as my elder law attorney, I would never have realized the full extent of my mother's rights and how I could advocate for her needs. My uninformed and misguided decisions could have negatively impacted my mother and myself, financially and personally, in profound ways.

Moreover, armed with the information and support I gained from the very first meeting with Michele and her team, I now understand that I am in control of what happens to my mother. Not the hospital, nor the nursing home. I am. There is a great sense of empowerment and peace that comes from an informed view gained by consulting an elder law attorney. Knowing my rights and taking the initiative to thoroughly do my own research eliminated the panic and greatly changed the course of events. I have Michele to thank for making me fully recognize the control I have over our circumstances.

In the end, it is not the pomp and circumstance of expensive décor and upscale architecture that makes my mother happy on a day to day basis. Although there is nothing inherently wrong with sophisticated interiors, what truly makes my mother content is the heartfelt efforts and care by professionals that spend their days assisting my mother and attending to her needs, as well as the culture of warmth and friendship they create everyday within the home itself.

Similarly, it is the heartfelt care and efforts by my elder law attorney, Michele Fuller, that cause her to stand out among other lawyers. I was lucky enough to be referred to someone who works above and beyond her title as an attorney, and it is reflected in her deep concern and thoughtful, informative conversations and direction. I wasn't merely informed as to what I should do; it was important to her that I fully understood why certain aspects of the plan needed to happen. Her efforts in doing so were not only for me to appreciate the course of action, but to ease my mind. The wellbeing of my mother and myself were of the utmost importance, and that is what causes Michele to stand out as exceptional in her field of expertise.

In the end, her brilliant and extensive planning, and deep concern, is what brought my mother and I through one of the toughest situations of our lives, a situation that was rapidly becoming dark and hopeless. For many in similar circumstances, their experiences are often laden with people who are crude, ill-intended, and thoughtless. However, my mother now lives with professionals that are highly respectful and who deeply care, much like Michele. Because of this, as of today, my mother lives with her dignity intact.

I am forever thankful to attorney Michele Fuller and her team. With her by my side throughout this challenging time, my mother has found grace in her life once again. I take solace in the knowledge that I have done my very best for her when she needed me most.

www.ingramcontent.com/pod-product-compliance
Lightning Source LLC
Chambersburg PA
CBHW060221050426
42446CB00013B/3130